F. S. Presbrey

Summer Paradise

F. S. Presbrey

Summer Paradise

ISBN/EAN: 9783744791472

Printed in Europe, USA, Canada, Australia, Japan

Cover: Foto ©Andreas Hilbeck / pixelio.de

More available books at **www.hansebooks.com**

A SUMMER PARADISE

COMPLIMENTS OF THE
DELAWARE & HUDSON R. R.,
CHAMPLAIN TRANSPORTATION, AND
LAKE GEORGE STEAMBOAT CO'S

A SUMMER PARADISE

FRANK PRESBREY

T HE beloved and venerated Bryant, in whose poems we find many songs to nature set in rhythmic metre, said:

"Go abroad upon the paths of Nature;
And when all its voices whisper, and its silent things
Are breathing the deep beauty of the world,
Kneel at its ample altar."

The Adirondacks may not have been the inspiration of these lines, but there is no spot where the voices of Nature whisper in sweeter cadence, or with more enticing or bewitching harmony of tone.

Silence and solitude appeal to most of us with a voice that is almost human. In it we recognize the vast domain of the world of matter, the sense of infinity lays hold of us, and a responsive chord goes out from our inmost soul, proclaiming in indisputable emotions our kinship with Nature. It is a dull soul which does not awaken to the glories of a magnificent sunset, or which is not stirred by the majesty of towering mountains, the deep solitude and stillness of the forest, or the dashing of the mighty waves of the sea upon the beach. Nowhere is Nature's "ample altar" more beautifully raised than in the great stretches of the North Woods. It is there that one may pitch his camp on the edge of some crystal lake, amid the stately monarchs of the forest, and enjoy for weeks at a time unbroken communion with Nature, undisturbed by the noise and strident calls of the work-a-day world. He may lay aside, as absolutely as if he were in another sphere, the cares and worries of busy commerce and the perplexities and annoyances of business. The bustle of the busy marts of trade may be forgotten, and he may grow strong and hearty, replenishing his wasting vitality with Nature's choicest and surest remedies.

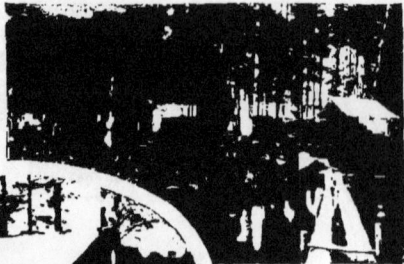

"He may pitch his camp on the edge of some crystal lake."

He may rest nights on a comfortable and sweet-scented couch made of fragrant balsam boughs, and be lulled to sleep by the wind humming its wordless songs through the feathery branches of the pines, to awaken full of renewed vigor to enjoy the luxury of a plunge in the cold water of the lake. He may partake of enviable meals—a tender bit of venison and a pan of brook trout, supplemented by flapjacks and maple syrup —all cooked à la Adirondack by one of the guides, who has a "knack," which when coupled with the surroundings brings out an appetite of which only a camper knows the length and breadth. After the morning meal is over the work or play of the day may begin. If the wind and sky are right he may slip off with one of the guides to a neighboring pond, where he knows of a "sly

hole" in which the ever wary brook trout may be tempted to rise for the fly, or he may troll in hope of getting one of the big lake trout, which are so plentiful, but which after the 1st of July are so illusive and sly. If he prefers, he may take his shotgun and pick up a few pheasants among the wooded patches which skirt the edge of every lake. If the camp has been properly located, he may nap or read in hammocks swung under the grand old monarchs of the woods and on the very edge of the clear, cool pond, whose surface, so closely protected from the winds by its boundaries of forest, will scarcely show more than a ripple on its placid bosom for days at a time. All these things, and many more too, may he enjoy. For if he is an ardent sportsman there is the excitement of the chase, when the deep baying of the hounds echoes and re-echoes against the mountain-sides—when it almost dies away as the noble buck rushes down into the valley over the range, only to spring into life and vigor again as he breaks across the nearest summit with the greedy pack in full cry at his heels. Evening comes early in these North Woods, as the mountains form a wall for the sun to hide behind as it sinks in the west,

"Where mountain streams babbling flow."

* * * "dying like a cloven king
In his own blood; the while the distant moon,
Like a fair prophetess, whom he has wronged,
Leans eager forward, with most hungry eyes,
Watching him bleed to death, and, as he faints,
She brightens and dilates; revenge complete,
She walks in lonely triumph through the night."

It is then that the camp fire with its huge logs piled high will blaze with

genial warmth. And where is the man or woman who, having once camped in the great North Woods, can efface the memories of those peaceful nights. As Murray says: "The memory is so truly a mirror that we may see as in a glass the trees and shores of lovely lakes, the wooded islands around which the waves run caressingly, beaches of glistening sand and ranges of lofty mountains." We ing notes of the songs whose melody drifted from the circle round the fire out over the tranquil and shadowy bosom of the lake. Sweet memories these, and the soul which does not beat responsive to their awakenings is dead indeed.

Picture in your mind a vast area whose surface is broken by numberless and mostly nameless mountains, clothed to their well-molded summits with the

We may see the forms and faces of those who have been our companions in forest life and wanderings "

may also see the cabins of bark, and tents made homelike. the camp-fires that crackle and blaze and send their twisting tongues of flames high up toward the swaying branches which shut out from view the starry firmament above. We may see too the forms and faces of those who have been our companions in forest life and wanderings. We hear again in mellowed tones the happy sounds of merriment and frolic, and listen to the echo- towering and stately pine and spruce. Imagine among these noble hills countless lakes of water so translucent as to be almost crystal, and into which the eye may penetrate to almost any depth; and on whose surface are reflected, as in a mirror, the darkened, graceful shadows of the mountain slopes. Imagine an atmosphere fragrant with the invigorating odor of the health-giving balsam, and so light and pure that the lungs seem suddenly to have increased to double their power, while one's vitality has taken on a renewed and strengthened life. Surround all of this with a framework of romance and the gentle grace of nature, and you have the Adirondacks.

Any one who imagines that America is lacking in that element of picturesqueness which attracts tens of thousands of

is an atmosphere about their grassy streets which reminds one of Goldsmith's "Sweet Auburn;" and their architecture, if not strikingly original, is of that rough simplicity so pleasing to the eye, and only the man who has travelled so much as to be possessed of the spirit of *ennui* can resist the dreamy beauties of these little hamlets on the hillsides.

It is scarcely more than a generation ago that the Adirondacks were known only by name, and their mountains, their lakes, and beautiful valleys were familiar but to the Indians, the trappers, and the few more hardy sportsmen who occasionally penetrated their depths.

In these days, however, all their attractive portions have been brought within easy access by the luxurious trains of the Delaware and Hudson Railroad and its connections, the Adirondack Railroad, the Chateaugay Railroad, and the

Americans to Europe every summer, can never have penetrated this beautiful Adirondack region. Here are combined all the charming scenic effects of Switzerland—a little less severe, perhaps, but all the more restful to the eye; here are found all the attractions of the lake region of Italy, for Como and Maggiore are no more lovely than Placid and Mirror. There is, to be sure, no Jungfrau or Matterhorn in the North Woods of the Empire State, but there is noble old White

"When the guides and hunters return to camp to count the trophies of the chase."

Face and Marcy, which, amid their surroundings, are as beautiful. There may be, perhaps, an element of novelty lacking in the Adirondack villages—such as pervades the hillside villages of Switzerland—they may be commonplace, but they are American, and add their quota of picturesqueness to the scene. There

Champlain Transportation Co. steamers. This great region, which is now to the East what the Yellowstone and Yosemite are to the West, is bounded by Lake George and Lake Champlain on the east, the St. Lawrence on the northwest, extending on the north to Canada, and on the south nearly to the Mohawk River. The moun-

tains rise from an elevated plateau of 15,000 square miles, in itself nearly 2,000 feet above the level of the sea. There are to be seen five distinct and well-defined parallel ranges running from southwest to northeast, and terminating on the eastern side in the rugged promontories which mark the western shore of Lake Champlain. The western range, called sometimes the Adirondacks and sometimes the Clinton, begins at the pass of Little Falls upon the Mohawk River, and stretches across the wilderness to the bold Trempleau Point at Port Kent on Lake Champlain.

Mount Marcy, called by the Indians Tahawus, meaning "sky piercer," and the loftiest summit of the Adirondack region, is 5,337 feet high, while Mounts Seward, McIntyre, and White Face, neighboring summits of Marcy, all exceed 5,000 feet. Recent surveys tell us that there are in the entire region over 500 distinct mountains, many of them as yet unnamed upon the maps of the region, but all massive and majestic in their proportions, and as a whole presenting one of the most magnificent scenic panoramas to be found in the world.

The Adirondack wilderness may be divided into three general divisions or systems, which taken collectively entertain the great bulk of visitors, and are representatives of the whole, namely, the Saranac and St. Regis waters of Franklin county, whose natural gateway is Plattsburg and Port Kent on Lake Champlain; the mountain region at Keene, North Elba, and Lake Placid, in Essex County, with entrance at Westport on Lake Champlain; and the Loon, Schroon, Blue Mountain, and Raquette Lakes country, with entrance from Saratoga over the Adirondack Railroad. Of these sections, the first mentioned has become the more widely celebrated as a region where fashion and fishing are admirably blended, and has its patrons who are looked for as regularly as the seasons. The second is perhaps a little less known, but its grand old mountains and winsome valleys have become world-renowned through the productions of great painters. The Schroon Lake region is not so wild but exceedingly popular. While possessing something of the characteristics of the others, each section has its own individual attraction, and while connected by natural highways and waterways over which the nomad often goes, they still,

"Where one may choose 'twixt lake and stream."

"Talking over the incidents of the chase on the way back to camp."

to a considerable extent, retain their individuality, and each is complete and sufficient unto itself. Keene Valley is a favored resort with artists and lovers of nature. Raquette Lake has the most elaborate, and the Upper Saranac the greatest number of private

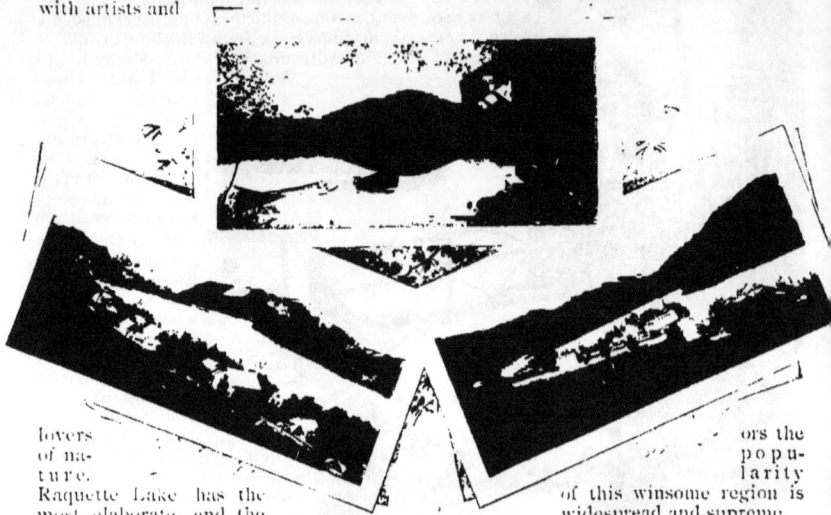

"There is a fascinating peace and tranquillity in the air."

camps occupied during the season. At intervals throughout the entire wilderness, all waiting with doors open to receive strangers, are places of entertainment, from the well-appointed hotel on the border to the rude log-house and open camp of the interior, the consideration being from $5 per week up to $3 to $5 per day. Freedom from rough and vicious characters is a peculiarity of the Adirondack region. Evil finds nothing congenial under its bright skies and in its pure, bracing atmosphere. Customs that obtain at other resorts are not held binding here. The fact of actual presence is accepted as a guaranty of the possession of those mutual sympathies and qualifications which, here at least, make the whole world kin, and make it possible for gentlemen to wear outing shirts and old hats, and ladies to travel without male escort from one end of the wilderness to the other. It is no uncommon thing for parties of ladies to make the tour of the woods accompanied only by the necessary complement of guides to furnish motive power, spending day after day in their boat and at night reaching one step farther in the extended system of hotels.

It is but quite recently that the many ideal attractions of the Adirondack mountains as a winter health and pleasure resort have come into prominence, although with summer visitors the popularity of this winsome region is widespread and supreme.

The great thoroughfare over which the travel into the Adirondacks goes is the Delaware and Hudson Railroad. Albany, N. Y., is its central point, and in this city are located its general offices. From here it stretches through a beautiful region southwest to Binghamton, N. Y., and Wilkes-Barre, Pa., and north through Saratoga and up past Lakes George and Champlain to the northern limits of the United States, its through trains running to Montreal. At Saratoga it connects with the Adirondack Railroad, which reaches a large portion of the North Woods, and at Plattsburg with the Chateaugay Railroad for many principal points in the Adirondacks. At Westport it connects with the excellent system of stage lines covering the central section. At Caldwell on Lake George and Fort Ticonderoga and Plattsburg on Lake Champlain it connects with the beautiful steamers of the Champlain Transportation Company and the Lake George Steamboat Company, the tickets of the rail and boat lines being interchangeable. The city of Albany, as has been said, is the central point in this great system, and is not only one of the oldest cities of America in point of settlement but one of the most attractive.

The Hotel Kenmore, at Albany, of which Mr. H. J. Rockwell is proprietor and Mr. F. W. Rockwell manager, is a

"The Kenmore is beautifully located in the centre of Albany's business district, and is very popular."

thoroughly modern house in all that that word implies. It is beautifully located in the very centre of Albany on the principal retail thoroughfare, and convenient to the State Capitol and the new depot. The Kenmore's wide popularity is due in no small degree to its liberal management, which has expended large sums of money in equipping the house with all appliances and luxuries which add to the comfort or convenience of guests. This house is one of the most thoroughly protected against fire in the State of New York, and is the rendezvous for the political as well as the fashionable and commercial travelling public.

The table at the Kenmore is not only abundantly but almost prodigally supplied with all the substantials and delicacies of the season, and all of its rooms, both for public and private use, are furnished in keeping with the high standard of the house. Those who appreciate the comforts of a good hotel will find them exemplified in the Kenmore.

Stanwix Hall, of Albany, of which Mr. C. Quackenbush is proprietor, is known the length and breadth of the country. It is one of the most comfortably equipped hotels in the State, and is conducted on both the American and European plans. It is the desire of the manage-

ment in all matters to satisfy the most exacting taste, and during the past two years the house has been thoroughly renovated and very many improvements have been made in order to more fully carry out this desire. New plumbing has been put in throughout the entire house, and an extensive and costly system of filtering the entire water-supply of the house has been introduced. Stanwix Hall is the nearest of any of the first-class hotels to the depots and steamboat landings, and enjoys a very large patronage.

The table at Stanwix Hall is maintained at the highest point of excellence, and special attention is paid to this feature of the house.

There is so much of interest to see in the capital of the Empire State that few people pass through without spending at least a short time in visiting those points of interest. Tourists going from New York, the West, or from any of the New England points to the Adirondacks pass through Albany, and a large number of these will be found registered at Stanwix Hall.

"Stanwix Hall at Albany is one of the most comfortably equipped hotels."

who prior to the war of the Revolution defended in Parliament the rights of the American colonists. Nearly a half hundred extensive coal-mines are located in the immediate neighborhood of Wilkes-Barre, and the amount of coal tonnage of the city runs into figures which are very impressive in magnitude. Upon this line of the Delaware and Hudson Railroad is also located the cities of Pittston and Scranton, the former being at the junction of the Susquehanna and Lackawanna rivers, and, like Wilkes-Barre, devoted to coal interests.

Scranton has enjoyed the distinction of having been called at various periods by more names than any other town in the United States. But notwithstanding, it has had many years of prosperous existence and is widely and justly celebrated because of its enormous iron-works, rolling mills, blast furnaces, and mines and manufacturing interests.

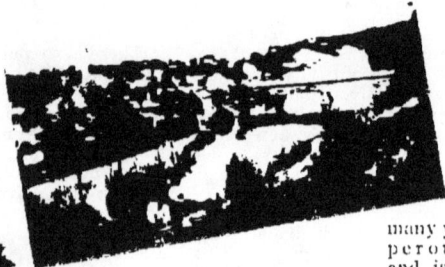

That portion of the D. & H. which, leaving Albany, runs southwest to Binghamton, branching at Nineveh and continuing to Wilkes-Barre, through Carbondale, passes through one of the most delightfully picturesque regions in the eastern country. There are attractive villages in which are exemplified the better phases of our American rural life, and there are many spots where Nature seems to have made a special effort to cluster attractive bits of scenery. Wilkes-Barre, the southwestern terminus of this division, is the commercial centre of the great anthracite coal region of the Wyoming Valley. This town bears the joint name of two distinguished Englishmen, John Wilkes and William Barre.

"The valley of the Susquehanna with its well-tilled farms and prosperous villages."

At Carbondale are located the very extensive car and machine shops of the D. & H. It is also the terminus of the Gravity Railroad, which belongs to the same system.

In describing this unique railroad the author of "Wonders and Curiosities of the Railway" says: "It lies among the picturesque Moosic Mountains, two thousand feet above the sea. The railroad fills up a gap seventeen miles long separating the mines from the mountain terminus of the canal. The hilly nature of the region determined the character of the railway. It consists of twenty inclined planes from one to four miles in length. From the summit to Carbondale there is an uninterrupted descent, down which the cars rush at a speed of sixty miles an hour. An enormous fan at the Summit's engine-house regulates the rate of descent by atmospheric pressure. In 1877 the first passenger cars were put on the road, to the great enjoyment of visitors and citizens. The ride is one of the most peculiar and exhilarating in the world. You are reminded of the magical car of the subterranean Egyptian temple described by Tom Moore in his 'Epicurean.' Here you are travelling for miles up hill and down, through beautiful scenery, and no visible agency to propel you. East and south the landscape stretches away for sixty miles; at the Shepherd's Crook you whirl around the summit of a gorge four hundred feet in depth, with a series of cataracts leaping down three hundred feet among the hemlocks, and the valley of the Lackawanna, spotted with towns and farms, stretching out far and wide in the distance. There is no dust, no smoke, no cinders, no whistle, no intrusive official; you only feel that some gigantic piece of clockwork is drawing you smoothly onward, and you lie back in your seat in tranquil enjoyment, and yield yourself to the novel illusion of magical power." A large amount of money is being spent in improving a natural park at Fairview, the highest point on the line.

"The ride over the Gravity Railroad is an inspiration."

About ten miles to the east of Binghamton, at Sanitaria Springs, N. Y., on the D. & H., is located the new Sanitarium and Hydrotherapium, one of the largest, best-equipped, and complete institutions of its class in the United States, if not in the world. Dr. S. Andral Kilmer, M.D., who is so extensively known as a successful physician in the treatment of chronic diseases, has expended enormous sums of money in the development of this enterprise, and the buildings are thoroughly equipped with the best systems of sanitation and ventilation. The location of the Sanitarium is peculiarly beautiful, the various structures being scattered about the hillside, and each, having been recently erected, is possessed of attractive architectural appearance. There are at the Sanitarium several mineral springs, one of which is sulpho-phosphate, the only spring of its kind in the world. Its medicinal properties are producing marvellous and beneficial results; and many obstinate cases of diseases, which have failed to respond to treatment in any other locality, have been treated here, where a corps of most efficient physicians are in daily contact with the patients. The buildings include everything which can be devised for the comfort and health of the guests and patients. They are equipped with electric lights, elevators, steam heat, and electric bells. All kinds of baths, sulphur, Turkish, Russian, pine needle, hemlock, balsam, electric, and Dr. Kilmer's new herbal and magnetic baths are administered under competent advice. Taking the Sanitarium as a whole, it is a model. The peculiar health-giving qualities of its waters, added to its delightful location among the Blue Hill Tunnel Ranges, 2,300 feet above the sea, the very competent medical attendants, reinforced by the wealth of Dr. Kilmer, who has spared no amount of money, have

" The new Sanitarium and Hydrotherapium at Sanitaria Springs is one of the largest institutions of its kind in America."

made it known the length and breadth of the land.

The Sanitaria and Hydrotherapium do not depend in their treatment solely on the uses, internally and externally, of waters, but comprehend a careful regulation of daily diet, prescribed recreation, rest, and whatever can be safely done by hygiene and medicine; nor does it limit itself to any one school of practice, but employs all known remedial agents, preferring Nature's remedies. It is conducted in winter and summer as a *distinctively health hydrotherapium*, alike homeful to all, whether the invalid wife or daughter of the millionaire or artisan.

On this division of the D. & H., and about 40 miles from Albany, is the wonderful Howe's Cave, the greatest in the world after the Mammoth Cave of Kentucky. It is full of weird attractions, and it is possible to travel over several miles of paths within it and not exhaust all its attractions.

Cooperstown, on Otsego Lake; Sharon Springs, the Baden-Baden of America; Unadilla, and many other charming resorts are on the line of the D. & H. between Albany and Binghamton. Full information may be had of the Passenger Department of the D. & H. at Albany.

The scenery of the valley of the Upper Hudson between Troy and Saratoga is bordered easterly by the distant range of the Green Mountains and a wide foreground of undulating hills. Westerly a continuity of high land limits the view of the open country be- yond. The landscape along the Hudson dispreads itself through brooky meadows, arable fields, and short stretches of woodland. As far as Mechanicville, the Rensselaer and Saratoga Rail-

Round Lake, three miles in circumference, is picturesquely environed by gently sloping hills, woody knolls, and grassy meadows. Long Lake, four miles westward, disembogues by an outlet into Round Lake, which discharges its water through Anthony's Kill into the Hudson, seven miles eastward.

The grounds of the Round Lake Association, about two hundred acres of land, lying west of the lake, are in the town of Malta, in Saratoga County, New York, nineteen miles from Troy, seven from Mechanicville, six from Ballston Spa, and thirteen from Saratoga Springs on the Delaware and Hudson Railroad The highway on the east side of the grounds runs through Maltaville, a mile northeast of them, and through Jonesville, three miles southwestward.

The sun-flecked depths of the cottage-clustered wood are entered by broad avenues diverging from the gateways at

road runs between the Champlain Canal and the Hudson. North of the village, the road, by a reverse curve like the letter S, bends westwardly around the south side of Round Lake, and passing the station extends northwesterly to Ballston Spa.

"The buildings of the Round Lake Association are attractive structures."

"Where the Hudson disperses itself through brooky meadows."

the passenger station on the east side of the railroad. Narrow lawns brightly bedded with flowers border these approaches and the paths extending from them. Beyond the prettily-built summer homes along the west side of the majestic grove appear others of varied architecture, embowered by the branches of the tall trees surrounding them. In the central part of this sylvan retreat is a large pavilion with thousands of sittings for the people attending the religious meetings, summer schools, Sunday-school assemblies, lectures, oratorios, exhibitions, and concerts held there in the summer. Conspicuously fronting the north lawn is the admirably arranged and finely furnished Hotel Wentworth. Farther northward, in a leafy recess of great oaks and fragrant evergreens, is the handsomely built Griffin Institute, which, in all its elaborate features, fitly expresses the unstinted generosity of the highly esteemed president of the Round Lake Association. East of the wood, on a rise of ground commanding a wide prospect of the surrounding country and an extended view of the lake, is the George West Museum of Art and Archæology, a finely proportioned structure, given the association by its generous treasurer. Garnsey Hall, on Whitfield Avenue, and Kennedy Hall, on Peck Avenue, are also attractive edifices, gifts of the two benevolent women whose names the well-planned buildings bear. Alumni Hall, on Whitfield Avenue, is also a noticeable structure.

A thorough system of sewerage is one of the arguments for the healthfulness of Round Lake Grounds. Added to this are the sparkling springs and rills which come from the sandhills on the west, furnishing the finest of cool pure water. All three augur well for the growing popularity of the place as a quiet, safe, moral, and intellectual resort. There are now planted here on a permanent basis the Round Lake Academy, a yearly institute; Round Lake Summer Musical Festival; Round Lake Ministers' Institute; Sunday-School Assembly; and Conference Camp-Meeting. Last, but not least, was the planting here

"And the buildings have been well planted for their uses."

of the Eastern New York Summer School for Teachers, under a corps of efficient directors, at the head of which is Prof. A. Falconer, of Waterford, N. Y.

There are at Round Lake some four hundred attractive and comfortable cottages and houses, and several pleasant hotels and boarding-houses, besides the above-mentioned Hotel Wentworth, and many people spend the entire summer season there, as at Round Lake there are found so many diversified pleasures.

Those desiring fuller or more complete information regarding the attractions of Round Lake and its work will receive it, and also a free journal, by addressing the Superintendent's Office, at Round Lake, Saratoga Co., New York.

"Every foot of the shore of Round Lake is attractive."

Amid all the rivalry of the innumerable places clamoring for popularity as summer resorts, regardless of the ever-changing fickleness of the public which has by turns stamped its seal of approval, now on one place and again on the other, fair Saratoga has reigned supreme as Queen of America's summer resorts. All the others have been and

must continue to be compared to her, and be content with the second place. She has fairly won and deservedly holds the title of the most popular and representative resort. For about Saratoga are clustered historical memories leading up to the establishment of American independence, as enduring as time, and these have been supplemented in more recent years by associations which have marked it as a summer capital where one is sure to find in the fullest degree a representation of the leading circles of wealth and refinement. To-day Saratoga is one of the most delightful little cities on the American continent, with a population all its own of about 12,000 and a summer population of 60,000 or more. It is located in the midst of the beautiful upper Hudson country, and in every direction run well-graded boulevards. The springs are among the natural curiosities of the world, and there are as many as twenty-eight within the limits of the city of Saratoga, all easily accessible from the hotels and residential districts.

Of all the springs which have made Saratoga famous, none has a wider or greater reputation than the Saratoga Vichy, which is a veritable geyser, the pressure of the natural carbonic acid gas being so strong that it forces the highly

"Some of the springs at Saratoga is more widely known than the Vichy."

charged mineral water out and throws it several feet into the air. The water from this celebrated spring is not saline but alkaline, and it is, therefore, exceedingly beneficial. The large quantity of bicarbonate of soda contained in it makes it of very great value in counteracting the acidity of the stomach and the blood. Its power of strengthening the digestive function and in eliminating the stubborn and dangerous diseases of the depurative organs is very great. Its value as a therapeutic agent is very well known, and it is sold throughout the civilized world. The appliances for bottling the water at the spring, just as it flows from the rock, are such as to preserve all of its natural carbonic acid gas, which gives it the same sparkling effervescence and delicious taste, even after it has been bottled for long periods. The Saratoga Vichy is a delicious beverage, refreshing and slightly stimulating, and its popularity is exceedingly great, not only as a pleasant table water, but a valuable remedy.

The American House at Saratoga is situated on Broadway, the main boulevard of the city, between the Grand Union and United States hotels, and its wide piazzas command opportunities for viewing the life and gayety of this celebrated resort. It is within two minutes' walk of the principal springs and Con-

"The American at Saratoga is a thoroughly well-appointed house."

gress Springs Park. The American is a thoroughly well-appointed house, excellently managed, and offers to visitors every attraction and comfort that can be found anywhere. The present season is its fifteenth, and throughout its entire existence it has maintained its present great popularity.

"The United States Hotel at Saratoga Springs which is so far-famed and popular."

The United States Hotel at Saratoga Springs is so far-famed and so thoroughly popular that it hardly seems possible to say anything new regarding it. It is one of the institutions of America. Within its walls gather each year thousands of the representatives of the world of fashion, wealth, and refinement. It is in itself a great social capital, and is on a scale so grand that its very magnitude is impressive. Within a court formed by three sides of the hotel is one of the loveliest private gardens in America, filled with beautiful fountains, the rarest of shrubs, and no more brilliant scene is to be found anywhere that is here presented each evening, when the park and the surrounding piazzas are thronged with the gay concourse of guests. The finest music is rendered morning, afternoon, and evening on the broad por-

ches, and even a glimpse of the brilliant scenes for which the United States Hotel is famous will long linger in the mind.

Its very immensity is a charm in itself, for there is in the great corridors, parlors, and dining rooms a sense of freedom from all restraint. It is like roaming about a great baronial palace, yourself a prince, with vistas through the hallways and from the windows on the one side of fairy-like gardens, with glis-

"Fairy-like gardens, with glistening fountains, and air fragrant with the verdure."

tening fountains, and the air fragrant with the verdure, and on the other, the gay boulevards of the city of Saratoga, alive with the handsome equipages and trappings of fashion and wealth. The cuisine of the United States is to the uninitiated a marvel, and to those accustomed to all the good things of life a joy and satisfaction.

The markets of New York are drawn upon heavily each day for all the luxuries and delicacies of the season, and the fertile country about Saratoga for vegetables and the dairy products for which this region is famous.

This hotel is one of the most perfectly appointed and beautiful in the world, and the visitor who spends a day, a month, or a season within its hospitable portals will ever recur with pleasure to the experience.

"Its spacious parlors with handsome furnishings."

There is no one summer resort in America where the names of the prominent hotels are more indissolubly associated with that of the town than in the case of Saratoga, for, take it where you will, whoever knows of Saratoga knows of its great hostelries. Congress Hall, one of the most famous and popular of the large number located at Saratoga Springs, was built shortly after the war, and occupies almost the entire square bounded by Broadway, East Congress, Spring, and Putnam streets. Its location is in the very heart of the fashionable part of Saratoga, and its great piazzas along the Broadway front are 250 feet in length, 20 feet wide, and at any hour of the day are gay with the wealth and fashion which gives Saratoga its prominence over any other resort in the United States. From the Broadway frontage there are two wings, 300 feet long, extending to Putnam Street, and between them a beautiful garden plot, filled with beautiful flowers and shrubbery and shade-trees. Wide porches surround this lovely park, and every morning and afternoon one of the largest bands, located in a central position, renders selections of the best class of music. Few more delightful spots could be found in which to pass an hour than in this beautiful park when the afternoon sun has left it in grateful shade, or the reflected evening lights from the hotel have added their brilliancy to the scene.

"Congress Hall is one of the great hostelries at Saratoga Springs, whose name and fame are world-wide."

There are, of course, to be found in Congress Hall all of the elegant and modern appointments which even the most exacting may require. Its beautiful dining rooms, halls, and parlors are models of their kind, and its culinary department is amply provided for the thousand guests which Congress Hall can accommodate. The most careful attention has been paid to the furnishing of the house, and its bedchambers and public rooms are models of comfort and luxury.

"The Floral Festival at Saratoga is its most attractive fête."

Worden's Hotel at Saratoga Springs is an all-the-year-round house, and is one of those comfortable, delightful places

"The Worden at Saratoga Springs is an all-the-year-round house."

where one may be certain of securing excellent accommodations. While the fame of Saratoga rests upon its being a summer resort, it is in fact one of the most delightful places to go in the winter season, and Worden's Hotel not only has a full complement of summer guests, but, after the great summer throngs have gone, maintains its popularity with those who are familiar with Saratoga when it is mantled with snow and when winter sports rule the day. Mr. W. W. Worden, the proprietor, is thoroughly alert to all that is modern in hotel-keeping, and this accounts in a large measure for the popularity of his house.

The Schroon Lake region and that beyond is the most accessible of any, and is as well one of the most beautiful in the North Woods. Schroon Lake is itself the largest lake in the Adirondacks, and is long, narrow, and crooked. It is entirely surrounded by graceful and lofty mountain peaks, which give it a wild and most impressive environment. Because it is so easily reached by rail and stage, many people of wealth and taste have fringed its picturesque shores with summer houses; and these people, as well as many others who are not so fortunate as to possess their own cottages or camps, come season after season to find that time does not wither nor custom stale the charm of its blue waters, the spicy, invigorating fragrance of its air, or its delicious restfulness.

The attractions of Schroon Lake from the fisherman's point of view are tempting. It has been well stocked with gamey lake trout, and many beautiful specimens of this delicious fish are caught each season. Black bass and pickerel are also

found plentifully, while the near-by ponds and streams and lesser lakes are filled with brook trout.

Schroon Lake and its surrounding region is reached by the Adirondack R.R., which, starting from the same station at which the Delaware and Hudson Railroad leaves its passengers in Saratoga, pursues a course a little west of north for sixty miles, to North Creek. Tourists going to Schroon Lake are met at Riverside Station and conveyed by comfortable stages, over winding roads through magnificent pine groves, to Pottersville, seven miles away, at which place they embark on the steamer, which proceeds up the lake, touching at intermediate points, to Schroon Lake Village, situated at the northern extremity of the lake. It is here that most of the hotels are located.

The village faces directly south, and is protected on the north by high mountains. This situation gives it an uncommonly moderate temperature for such a latitude, and makes it a delightful place in which to tarry after the season has closed at other less favorably located spots in the mountains.

There are many beautiful drives in the Schroon Lake region, the favorite routes being to Paradox Lake, where excellent trout dinners are served, and to Pyramid Lake and Brant's Lake. Among other points worthy a visit is the old staging house, nine miles north of Schroon Lake, one of the first houses built in the mountains, and situated on the old post road from Albany to Montreal. From Riverside, where tourists leave the railway, a stage also runs to Chestertown, a distance of six miles. Schroon, Brant, Friend, and Loon Lakes are all within

"Schroon Lake is the largest of all those in the Adirondack region."

a radius of five miles of Chestertown, and are accessible by good roads through an interesting region.

"The Club at Brant Lake is one of the attractive features of this beautiful spot."

its course the offerings of many smaller streams, emerging from the wilderness; thence it turns to the east, and, after its uncertain course of almost 100 miles, reaches the great cataract at the prosperous city of Glens Falls.

Glens Falls is a very prosperous little city of 12,000 inhabitants and the centre of large manufacturing interests, made possible by the superb water-power furnished by the Hudson River, which at this point makes a descent of 56 feet over rocky falls.

The most famous scenic attraction of this place is the cave made memorable in Cooper's novel, "The Last of the Mohicans." There is an air of general thrift about Glens Falls which is noticeable even to the most casual visitor. The city has a particularly cleanly appearance, and there is through its residential section a wealth of broad velvety lawns and noble shade-trees, among which are many notably attractive and beautiful homes.

Those stopping at Glens Falls will find the Rockwell House, of which Mr. C. L. Rockwell is proprietor, very pleasantly located on the chief business thoroughfare of the city in the very centre of the business portion. The Rockwell is one of the best

One of the most delightful spots on the Adirondack Railroad, and located in the very heart of the Adirondack Mountains, is Brant Lake. It is reached by a stage from the Riverside station. The lake is six miles long, and located upon it is the Brant Lake Club, of which Mr. D. G. Yuengling, Jr., of New York, is president, and Mr. John J. Lenehan secretary. It is equipped with every convenience and is within easy driving distance of Lake George, Schroon Lake, Friends' Lake, and all the other delightful and charming resorts of this region. The scenery all about is unsurpassed in beauty, grandeur and variety, and the roads, along which charming drives may be had, are perfect. Black bass and pickerel abound in the lake, which has been thoroughly stocked, and there is excellent trout fishing in the mountain streams near by. The post-office address of the club is Horicon, Warren County, New York.

From its source in the uttermost recesses of nature's own domain, the magnificent Hudson bounds into life through a thousand crystal springs, and by tortuous courses crosses Warren County, receiving the water of Schroon Lake, and continuing first southward, receives in

"Those stopping at Glens Falls will find the Rockwell House pleasantly situated."

conducted houses in New York, every attention being paid to those travelling for pleasure as well as for business.

There are few American lakes invested with richer historical associations than Lake George, for on its calm bosom and along its indented borders many sanguinary battles were stubbornly fought in Colonial times. Hereabouts Lords Amherst and Abercrombie, Montcalm and Rogers, Howe and Rigaud, Jacques and Williams met in mortal combat. There were long periods, before Hudson ascended the American Rhine, when on Lake George the Indians quietly speared the fish. Then came decades when the rattle of musketry and the boom of the cannon from the gunboats of Rogers and Putnam told of execution being accomplished among the canoes of the treacherous savages. All along its shores fierce wars were fought by the English, French, and aboriginal tribes. About the ruins of Forts William Henry, George, and Gage tragic memories thickly cluster, and the site of these historic earthworks are all within a mile of the Fort William Henry Hotel.

Nothing but ill luck betided the English in this section of the country. In 1757 the French and their Indian allies attacked Fort William Henry, at the head of the lake, which was held by a small garrison of English troops under Colonel Munro, who, after gallantly defending the post until their ammunition was exhausted and half of their guns burst, or otherwise rendered useless, surrendered to the French General Montcalm, the same who afterward met death so bravely upon the Plains of Abraham while defending Quebec against the onslaught of General Wolfe. The story of the massacre which followed the surrender has been often and vividly told, and generally with much exaggeration. Bloody Pond, a few miles from Fort William Henry, is still pointed out to the tourist and to the person fond of accepting tales as told to the marines. It is said to be the spot into which were incontinently thrown the bodies of pretty much all of the garrison surrendered by Colonel Munro, several hundred in all, while as a matter of historical fact not more than thirty were killed in the fight.

Speaking of the lake and of the events preceding the bloody scenes enacted at its head nearly a hundred and forty years ago, George Bancroft, the historian, has said: "How peacefully rest the waters of Lake George between their ramparts of hills; in their pellucid depths the cliffs and the hills and the trees trace their

"How peacefully rest the waters of Lake George between the ramparts of its hills."

images and the beautiful region speaks to the heart, teaching affection for nature. As yet not a hamlet rose on its margin, not a straggler had thatched a log hut in its neighborhood; only at its head, near the centre of a wider opening between the mountains, Fort William Henry stood on its banks, almost on a level with the

quisite pleasure, to breathe the invigorating atmosphere of the adjacent mountains is health-giving and health-restoring, to even exist here during the summer season is unalloyed joy.

The human interest in the lake and its vicinity affords one of the chief charms. Every corner has its historic legend or incident. These a hundred years have very often changed somewhat from the original versions and thrown into mellow perspective. The student of folk-lore might gather here many interesting tales and ballads from the old residents, handed down by mouth from colonial days when they were current and the heroes they celebrated were living men.

" There are many beautiful inland sheets of water, both in this country and in the old world, but never one that was fairer than Lake George."

lake. Lofty hills overhung and commanded the quiet scene, for the heavy artillery had not as yet accompanied war parties into this wilderness." And today just as " peacefully rest the waters of Lake George between their ramparts of hills," and just so to-day " in their pellucid depths the cliffs and the hills and the trees trace their images, and the beautiful region speaks to the heart, teaching affection for nature." Naught has been changed in that respect since those early days of which the venerable historian wrote, but in other ways the changes have been marvellous. Where " not a hamlet rose" or a " straggler had thatched a log hut," in the days of long ago, have been erected stately hotels, lovely summer homes and prosperous villages. There are many beautiful inland sheets of water, both in this country and in the old world, but never one that was fairer or whose natural surroundings were more picturesque than this one lying so close to our homes. To see it for the first time is a revelation, to glide over its waters and to wind in and out among its hundreds of rocky islands is ex-

Dunham Bay is thought by Dr. Eggleston to be the place where General Montcalm secreted his army of French and Indians with a view to surprising Fort William Henry, before the final attack. Parkman, in his Life of Montcalm, has given a graphic series of pictures of the lake in that struggle, and Cooper, in his story of the Mohicans, has immortalized the locality. On the lake just above the bay is the spot where Leatherstocking, Chingachgook, and Uncas were pursued in canoes and fought the Indians after the massacre of Fort William Henry. The cave where they took refuge with the daughters of Colonel Monro is still shown

" With dainty islands crowded close together."

at Glens Fallsas if the incident were a

"Looking off across the lake toward the graceful outlines of Black Mountain."

one of the most convenient and most delightful spots on the lake. Its location from a scenic point of view is as near ideal as can be, and the Horicon Improvement Company has done and is doing a great deal to add to the many advantages of the place. This enterprising company, in addition to owning and operating the old and ever-popular Lake House, which looks down through a lovely grove over wide-stretching lawns to the lake on one side, and faces the village street of Caldwell on the other, operates the Prospect Mountain House. This house has been built on the very summit of the majestic mountain of that name, which rises directly back of the village, and from which a most magnificent view embracing Lake George

reality, and the name of Horicon, which Cooper sought to bestow on the lake, lingers affectionately among its associations. Had Cooper wished to make a more exact historical novel he would have had abundant material in the daring feats and escapes of the intrepid Rogers, the captain of the lake riflemen during the French and Indian war. Rogers was one of the characters of that war, as he was one of the first of the great native Indian fighters of this country. He has left his name on many a story of Lake George, but he lost the opportunity of enrolling it among the Revolutionary patriots when he became a rabid Tory.

"Where the pretty summer homes and settlements grace the wooded shores."

Lake George is located in the St. Lawrence water-shed and empties into Lake Champlain, which also flows northward. It has as its chief town Caldwell, which is located directly at the head of the lake. Here the steamers connect with the trains of the Delaware and Hudson Railroad, which, leaving the main line at Port Edward, run to Caldwell, the line terminating upon the large pier, and the trains stopping directly at the side of the steamers.

People who are thoroughly informed as to the various beauties and attractions of Lake George appreciate the fact that the picturesque village of Caldwell, is

and the Hudson Valley may be had. Northward may be seen every prominent Adirondack peak, and down at the foot of the mountain, nestling amid a myriad of

"The Canoeing Association make it a rendezvous every year."

"From the porches of the Lake House at Caldwell a lovely vista of the lake is had through the trees."

trees, is the quiet, peaceful little village of Caldwell, hugging close to the western shore of the lake. A cable road longer in point of altitude and higher than either that at the Catskills, on Lookout Mountain in Tennessee, or at Pasadena, California, has been built up the side of the mountain, extending from the lake shore to the very summit. This road has been constructed by the Otis Engineering and Construction Company, and the cars are operated between the Lake House and Caldwell and the Prospect Mountain House, far above it on the top of the mountain, at short intervals.

The Lake House has, during the past season, been entirely remodelled, and in its equipment is as absolutely modern and metropolitan as it is possible to make a summer hotel. In its natural location there are few houses that excel it. Its grounds reach to the pebbly shores of the lake, and a number of handsome cottages surround the hotel proper, giving it a delightful colony effect. The drives about Caldwell are far-famed, especially those

over the magnificent graded boulevard to Warrensburg and up the western shore.

The Prospect Mountain House at the upper end of the long cable, which has fairly scorned in its construction the ragged sides of the mountain, is under the same management as the Lake House, and guests at one house may have the privileges of the other. It possesses all the agreeable features of club life, with private dining-rooms, and also a large restaurant open to the air on either side, or glass-enclosed, as the condition of the weather may make desirable; this is conducted on the European plan.

The other terminus of the steamer's trip is Baldwin, at the foot of the lake. This is the terminus of the Fort Ticonderoga branch of the Delaware and Hudson Railroad, and passengers going down Lake George by steamer make close connections there with the beautiful trains of this line for Lake Champlain resorts, Ausable Chasm, the Adirondacks, Montreal, and all Canadian points.

The trip down Lake George from Caldwell to Baldwin challenges in its every point of scenic beauty any other trip of

"The cable road runs from the village of Caldwell to the summit of Prospect Mountain."

equal length on the American continent. From time almost immemorial, poets and writers have apostrophized Lake George and laid their literary tributes, in prose and verse, upon its altar. Between the great ridges of mountains which close in upon its sides for its entire length

"Those who are informed consider Caldwell one of the most delightful places."

there lies a lake whose crystalline depths reflect so perfectly the blue azure of the sky that as it sparkles in the sunlight it almost reverses, and equals in brilliancy, the blue dome of the heavens above. Dotting its limpid surface are more than three hundred rocky and wooded islands, so closely crowded together in some parts of the lake that a pilot's utmost skill is required to guide the great white steamers between them. Many of these islands have been made attractive by quaint and slightly cottages, while others, belonging to the State and being free to all comers, have been made temporary homes by summer campers, who have spread their tents under the dense foliage, to enjoy, free from the conventionalities of hotel life, unrestrained communion with nature.

As if jealous of the approaches of the grim old mountains, the lake has, in many instances, crowded itself between them, and thus have been formed some of the loveliest of bays, where, protected from the winds and shaded by the wide-spreading trees along their edges, acres of water-lilies have claimed the domain as their own and spread over the tranquil water a carpet of leaf and blossom of nature's

own design, beautiful beyond description. It is in these sequestered, lovely spots that we may find the very acme of human rest. Here we may realize the delights of the spirit of *dolce far niente*, and may rest for hours beyond the reach of human voice under the shade of friendly boughs to dream or read, unmindful of the world, forgetful of care, forgetful of all except the beauty of nature's inner labyrinths.

The two well-appointed steamers, *Horicon* and *Ticonderoga*, or "Ti," as it is familiarly called, on their journey down the lake, make a score of stops, and cross and re-cross the lake many times. At each of these landing-places are hotels of greater or less importance, all with characteristic attractions and filled with summer guests. The very stopping at these landings is a source of diversified pleasure to the tourists, as at each wharf is found a gay group of summer campers who rally there at boat-time, as the villagers were wont to do around the country store when the daily stage arrived.

On the western shore of the the lake, six miles below Caldwell, and almost hemmed in by the mountains at its rear, stands the deservedly

"From the spacious porches of the Marion House there is a wide view of the lake."

popular Marion House. From its wide porches or beautiful lawn a view of almost the entire length of Lake George may be had. The steamers stop directly in front of the house, and there is for the use of the guests a large fleet of row-boats and two beautiful steam yachts, the *Rachel* and *Marion*. The table is supplied with the purest and freshest of farm products, and butter, milk and cream are supplied by the drove of Jersey cows which is one of the famous features of the place. Fine roads lead from the hotel, and good saddle-horses and stylish turn-outs are supplied to guests, who may also charter for special excursions the tally-ho coach, *Marion*. Almost every room in the house furnishes a lake view, although the mountain view from the western windows is quite as beautiful. The house is supplied with electric bells and lighted with gas and electricity. There are elevators, and the drinking water is brought from a large spring far up the mountainside.

In the heart of that portion of Lake George where the mountains are the wildest and the most rugged, and but six miles from Fort Ticonderoga, with its historic associations, is the Rogers Rock Hotel. It occupies a bold promontory just to the north of the famous Rogers Slide, where tradition has it that the general of that name slid down its smooth and precipitous face onto the ice of the lake to escape the Indians. On the summit of the mountain above the hotel the Rev.

" In the heart of that portion of Lake George where the mountains are the wildest is the Rogers Rock Hotel."

Joseph Cook has erected an observatory and a summer home, surrounded by a large and beautiful natural park. A well-made path leads to it directly from the hotel, thus making this observatory one of the popular places of resort, as the views from it take in the wildest range of lake and mountain scenery. The best

fishing grounds on the lake are in the neighborhood of the Rogers Rock Hotel, which has all of the requisites of an ideal summer home. The draining and sanitary arrangements are modern and perfect, and the table is in every feature excellent. The steamers on the lake all stop at the wharf of the hotel, and it is thus easy of access. Mr. T. J. Treadway is the manager, and Mr. W. D. Treadway proprietor, the post office address being Rogers Rock, Essex Co., N. Y.

"The Lake View House at Bolton, Lake George, is a pleasant place to tarry."

Bolton has long been known as one of the chief resorts of Lake George, and it has won distinction because of its beautiful—in fact, ideal—location on Parodi Point. Upon a wooded headland, and within one hundred feet of the pebbly edge of the lake, stands the Lake View House, of which Mr. R. J. Brown has been the proprietor ever since the house was opened in 1875. There is found in the Lake View one of the most comfortable and home-like summer hotels, a place where it is a pleasure to stay, and where within the easiest reach may be enjoyed all the various attractions of Lake George. This hotel accommodates about one hundred and fifty people, and the house is exceedingly well built and delightfully furnished. It is in the centre of the famous fishing district, and all about it are delightful opportunities for either sport or pleasure. A steam ferryboat plies between the hotel and the Bolton landing.

Lake Champlain, which runs within elongated and mostly narrow confines for one hundred and

twenty - s i x miles, almost north a n d south, divides

for this distance the States of New York and Vermont. South of Fort Ticonderoga, which is its southern terminus in a commercial sense, it is contracted between low and swampy shores, appearing to the eye more like a river than a lake, and at some points being scarcely 500 feet across. To the northward of Fort Ticonderoga, however, it broadens into a wide lake, reaching out at Burlington to a width of 10 miles, and, beyond this, to 15 miles, but with many intervening islands. In character Lake Champlain is vastly different from the smaller but no less beautiful Lake George. One is a picture and the other a miniature, both perfect in their way. If Champlain were human, one might say

smiles are found in the wide-stretching and pastoral hills to the eastward. The north winds, too, are apt to work it into an angry mood, and while it is never treacherous, it is far more apt to be rough and inhospitable than its more gentle companion, Lake George. Like the latter, it is rich in islands and there are no more beautiful trips upon inland seas than may be enjoyed upon the commodious and modern steamboats *Vermont* and *Chateaugay*, of the Champlain Transportation Company, which make the round trip of the lake daily, touching at all points.

The tourists on the Delaware and Hudson Railroad may, if they prefer, make the journey either way between Fort Ticonderoga to Plattsburg or Hotel Champlain by steamer instead of rail, as the tickets are good either way. Fort Ticonderoga, from which point the steamers leave, is as indissolubly associated with early American history as any other point on the continent. Upon the summit of Mt. Defiance, which stands directly to the west side of the railroad, Burgoyne, in July, 1777, planted his heavy battery and began the bombardment of the fort whose picturesque ruins still crown the summit of the

that it was petulant and smiling by turns, for upon one shore its precipitous and rocky promontories give it its frowns, while its

"Fort Ticonderoga is indissolubly connected with America's history."

rocky peninsula north of the steamer's pier. This was a natural location for such a stronghold, being bounded upon three sides by water, and on the fourth by a swamp. A little to the southeast, upon a high point, are the remains of the Grenadiers' Battery, still well preserved. The first defensive works on this point were built in 1690; and in the year following Major Schuyler here brought together the Christian and Mohawk forces which met their defeat at La Prairie. Almost three-quarters of a century after this, Baron Dieskau took possession of the fortification, and in the year following Montcalm with a large French army occupied it and gave the name of Fort Karillon to the extensive works which he built. Three years later, General Abercrombie, in command of 16,000 troops, made a vigorous attack upon the fort, but after a bloody fight was repulsed, the French losing 380 men and the Anglo-American army 1,942, the gallant Lord Howe being among those killed in this action. In 1758 Lord Amherst, with 11,000 men and 54 cannon, drove the French from the place, after they had burned the barracks and exploded the powder-magazine. From that time until the 10th of May, 1775, quiet reigned; but upon that day, Ethan Allen and Benedict Arnold, commanding their 85 New England men, surprised and captured the fort. In 1777 General St. Clair, with 3,446 men, held the fort, but Burgoyne, having advanced from Canada, succeeded through the bombardment from Fort Defiance in rendering the fort untenable. Ten weeks later the outworks of Fort Ticonderoga, with 200 *batteaux*, or war-vessels, and their cannon, and nearly 300 prisoners were captured by 1,000 New England troops which Colonel Brown led against the fortress, and the 100 American prisoners were liberated. A few weeks later the fort was dismantled, but in 1780 was reoccupied for a short period by General Haldemand, but since that time has been deserted. Eight miles above Fort Ticonderoga at Crown Point, which is in these modern days quite an iron manufacturing centre, the ruins of an old fortress may be seen upon a promontory between Lake Champlain and Bulwagga Bay. A fine stone lighthouse marks the point, but otherwise it is abandoned to its ancient ruin, the ramparts of which are fully half a mile around, twenty-five feet high and with the same thickness, being faced with stone. This fort, which was originally erected upon Pitt's orders

"Where placid bays indent the shores."

by Lord Amherst, is said to have cost the British ten millions of dollars.

In 1775 Warren's Green Mountain Boys captured the fort with its 14 guns; and in 1777 Burgoyne made the fort his chief depot of supplies in his advance on Albany. The old ramparts are overgrown with dense thickets and many blood-red thorn-apple trees. These are to be found nowhere else in the State, and are said to have been brought from France.

Fort Henry, a prosperous town located upon the shore of the lake at Bulwagga Port, eighteen miles above Ticonderoga, is the centre of the extensive iron mines thereabouts, and several great blast furnaces have been erected near the steamer's landing.

"Along the rocky shores of Lake Champlain with their weather and wave-battered faces."

Westport, eleven miles beyond, is charmingly situated on Westport Bay (called "Baie du Roche Fendu" on the wide—which is adjacent to the town, was the boundary between the territory of the Mohawks and the Algonquins, whose

"Westport overlooks the fairest portion of Lake Champlain."

old maps), overlooking the fairest portion of Lake Champlain. This was the scene of Gen. Benedict Arnold's famous fight with the *Congress* on October 13, 1776, on which he succumbed to the superior force of Captain Pringle and the British ships, and running the *Congress* galley and four gondolas into a small bay directly opposite Westport, burned them to the water's edge. Some of the cannon and many pieces of the famous ship have been taken from the lake.

This prosperous little town is in itself an important summer resort, but is known chiefly because of its superb situation as one of the principal gateways

"Here also is the Westport Inn, surrounded by many charms."

to the Adirondack region. It, too, has many historical associations, as Split Rock— a remarkable cliff, separated from the mountain by a deep cleft twelve feet

territories were occupied by the English and French respectively. In 1710 it was acknowledged by the Treaty of Utrecht as the limit of the English dominions, and in 1760 it was officially designated as the boundary between New York and Canada; but years subsequently the Americans passed it under arms and won the territory for 77 miles to the north.

The constantly increasing number of visitors to Westport—attracted thither by its historical associations, no less than by its beautiful location and an equable climate—find there a most comfortable hotel, "The Westport Inn," to which summer visitors return year after year, accompanied by friends to whom the story of Westport beauty has been told and retold.

Elizabethtown has been called, and very properly, the inner gateway of the Adirondacks; and this charmingly situated little town, with its environs of green hills and its background of graceful mountain peaks, is a fitting introduction to the wild grandeur of the country beyond, the land of shimmering lakes and solitude.

From Westport, which may be termed the outer gateway of the North Woods, the drive of eight miles to Elizabethtown through the Raven Pass on the comfortable tally-ho stages is one long to be recalled in pleasant memory.

There are few travellers who can resist the temptation to tarry for a few days at Elizabethtown, exploring the wonders of the region beyond.

Here he may study and enjoy the mountains which have as many moods as the sea; he may see their long dense shadows in the early morn, outlined with greater intensity in the deep gorges and ravines which the convulsions of nature have left as scars on the mountainsides.

At Elizabethtown is the ever-popular Windsor Hotel, with Mr. Orlando Kellogg as proprietor. Upon the pages of its register have been subscribed the names of thousands of people known to

"There are few who can withstand the temptation to spend a few days at Elizabethtown."

"The Windsor Hotel is the social center of Elizabethtown."

the world of letters, politics, and fashion. Elizabethtown is the tourist centre of the beautiful and unequalled Keene Valley, and the Windsor Hotel is the social centre of Elizabethtown. The Windsor coaches meet all trains and boats at Westport, and connect with stages to Keene Valley, Cascade Lakes, North Elba and Lake Placid. Private teams will be provided when requested. A delightful place at which to spend a longer or a shorter period, as it is within easy reach, by the best drives, of many of the most attractive spots in the Adirondacks. Elizabethtown is in itself a most charming village, and is within eight hours of New York, four hours from Albany, and three from Saratoga. The hotel itself is perfectly appointed and unexceptionably managed. It has every convenience which may add to the com-

fort and pleasure of existence. A handsome four-in-hand brake makes two trips daily from the Windsor through the surrounding mountains, and the livery attached to the house is abundantly supplied with saddle and driving horses. The table at the Windsor is not excelled anywhere, as the proprietor is the owner of one of the largest and best-appointed farms in northern New York, from which the table is supplied with fresh butter, cream, eggs and vegetables. Professor Mason, the analytical chemist, has pronounced the drinking water at Elizabethtown one of the purest waters he has ever analyzed.

Mr. Kellogg has had twenty-five years' experience in the hotel business at Elizabethtown, and it is doubtful if any man in America is better qualified to meet the requirements of summer guests. He is also proprietor of the Mansion House, Elizabethtown, of which his son-in-law Mr. C. A. Ferris, is the manager. The drive from Elizabethtown to Lake Placid is

"Where John Brown's body lies mouldering in the grave."

one of about
thirty miles; ev-
ery rod of the dis-
tance, every new
view opened up
at each turn in
the road, is full
of beauty. At
Keene Post-office
the east branch
of the Ausable
River is crossed,
and then begins
the climb along
the steep sides
of Pitchoff Moun-
tain to the series
of narrow ponds
known as the Cas-
cade Lakes. A
few rods across

"Keene Valley has no equal in America, if in the world, for picturesque loveliness and romantic beauty."

them the side of Long Pond Mountain
rises directly over the water, and as the
turn is made around the western end of
Pitchoff Mountain, the Giant of the Valley
springs into full view. Then there come
in rapid succession views of Wolf's Jaws,
Saddleback, Haystack, March, Colden,
McIntyre, and Wallface.

Descending into the valley of the west
branch of the Ausable, the road passes
the fields which John Brown cleared for
the use of the negroes before he made
his celebrated raid upon Harper's Ferry
which resulted in his death. One may

also see the old shingled cottage in the
distance, and the veteran's remains are
buried close by it. The village of North
Elba is in view five miles before it is
reached, and Lake Placid, perhaps three
miles beyond. At North Elba the west
branch of the Ausable is crossed and the
ascent made to Lake Placid Post-office,
which is really upon Mirror Lake.

Whiteface, which watches over Lake
Placid with majestic presence, is among
the highest of the Adirondacks. A wonderful view of Lake Champlain is had
from the summit, although it is forty
miles away. Un-
der favorable
weather condi-
tions Montreal and
the St. Lawrence
River can be seen
with a glass. Sev-
enty lakes, scat-
tered in all direc-
tions, may be seen
without a glass.
Lake Placid,
which is the most
beautiful of them
all, is the strategic
point of the whole
Adirondack re-
gion. As he looks
from Placid to the
southward, Sew-
ard, Wallface, Mc-
Intyre, Colden,
Marcy, Saw-teeth,
Gothic, and Am-
persand moun-
tains range them-
selves from west

"Here the mountains are rugged and bold, and clothed to their very summits with primeval forests."

"In the midst of the most sublime of the Adirondack scenery."

to east while off at the extreme right the Giant peeps out from the rear of Pitchoff and indicates the location of Keene Valley.

In the heart of beautiful Keene Valley stands St. Hubert's Inn, in the midst of the highest mountains and the most sublime of the Adirondack scenery. Keene Heights, upon which the Inn stands, is a broad plateau entirely surrounded by mountains clothed to their summits with primeval forests, and is in itself so elevated that it does not have the impression of being shut in.

The Adirondack Mountain Reserve, covering forty square miles of territory, immediately adjoins that of the hotel. Within this Reserve are the two beautiful Ausable Lakes and many trout streams. The guests of St. Hubert's are given permits to fish within its limits, and its many beauties are free to the guests of the Inn.

Dr. E. G. Janeway, of New York, a well-known expert, pronounces the air at Keene Heights particularly beneficial to those suffering from hay fever or asthma, while Stoddard, whose guide book of the Adirondacks is a classic in its way, says that "the scenery about St. Hubert's Inn, down the Keene Valley and up from the Adirondack Mountain Reserve, including the famous Ausable Lakes, is grand beyond description and Swiss-like in its beauty." No less an authority than Charles Dudley Warner has said of these lakes that "In the sweep of their wooded shores and lovely contour of the lofty mountains that

"The Ausable Lakes, the most charming of any in America."

guard them, they are probably the most charming in America."

St. Hubert's Inn is new, fresh, and attractive, modern in construction and thoroughly complete in every particular. There are surrounding it eighteen cottages, and thus is formed a complete colony with a social life as characteristic as it is charming. All of the vegetables, milk, cream and eggs come from Orlando Beede's farm in the valley.

Attached to St. Hubert's Inn is a casino for various entertainments, and a well-equipped livery stable attached to the Inn.

Messrs. Beede and Houghton are the proprietors. The post-office is named Beede's, and is located in the house.

"The view from St. Hubert's Inn is fascinating.

The Stevens House, which is the great social centre of the Lake Placid region, is picturesquely located, on an elevation commanding one of the most magnificent seaumont, the new hotel at Lake Placid. It overlooks both Mirror Lake and Lake Placid, and offers from its piazzas and windows some of the fairest and most

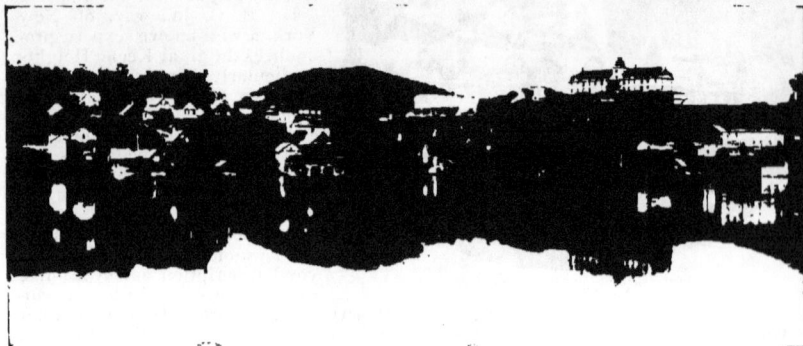

"From one side of the Stevens House may be seen Mirror Lake, and from the other, the ever beautiful Lake Placid."

of the many views which are afforded in this region. Its main floor is 2,063 feet above tide-water, and from one side of the hotel may be seen Lake Placid, and on the other Mirror Lake. There is no hotel in the Adirondacks which commands grander or lovelier views. The four highest mountains in the State stand out in full view from the porches of the hotel. The Stevens House is finished throughout in hard wood and handsomely furnished. Its ideal location makes every room a front room, and, unlike many of the summer hotels, its bedchambers are all large and each has two windows. Messrs. J. A. and G. A. Stevens are the owners and managers, and what Lake Placid is to the Adirondacks, the Stevens House is to Lake Placid.

Of all the Adirondack hotels none have a more ideal location than the Ruis-

extensive views. It is a modernly equipped hotel in every respect and under the management of Mr. T. Edmund Krumbholz has become a favorite

"The mountains are reflected in Mirror Lake with vivid distinctness."

stopping-place with the large number of Adirondack visitors who return to the Ruisseaumont after a tour through the mountains with the feeling that no other hotel can quite take its place. Although luxurious in its furnishings and with every convenience for the comfort and well-being of its guests, it yet retains that homelike character so often lacking at the great resort hotels of the country. The Ruisseaumont opens about the first of June, when the country is the most beautiful, and remains open until late in the fall. It has ample accommodation for two hundred guests. Further information will be furnished on application to the manager at Lake Placid.

"The Ruisseaumont has become a favorite stopping-place."

The Grand View Hotel at Lake Placid, of which an illustration appears on this page, is one of the newest and most mod- season on the 22d of June, and rates may be had by addressing The Grand View Hotel Company, Lake Placid, New York.

"The Grand View Hotel on Lake Placid is new and occupies a commanding view of Lake Placid and its surrounding mountains."

ern houses in the Adirondacks. It was built about two seasons ago and comfortably accommodates two hundred and fifty people. The house is built upon a commanding situation furnishing a combined view of mountain and lake. The office of the house is the largest in the Adirondacks, is handsomely furnished, and is very much used as a social-room by the ladies and gentlemen. The ball-room is forty by fifty feet, the same as the office; and the parlor is a separate room by itself and opens on three sides with broad verandas. The music of the house is under the direction of Professor Dubois, of Brooklyn, and three concerts are given each day. There is every facility at the Grand View for enjoying to the fullest extent life in the Adirondacks—out of

"The Algonquin on lower Saranac Lake."

doors there are tennis and base-ball grounds, and indoors there are billiards and pool. The Grand View opens this

Good roads through one of the most beautiful sections of the Adirondacks, from Lake Placid to Saranac Lake, present an opportunity for an ideal stage ride, but for tourists who desire to travel in a more comfortable and rapid manner a well-equipped railway has recently been constructed. This line, The Saranac & Lake Placid Railway, makes direct connection at Saranac Lake with all the trains of the Chateaugay line and brings the entire Lake Placid and Mirror Lake section within easy reaching distance of all points on the D. & H. system via Plattsburgh. At Saranac Lake, the terminus of the Chateaugay line, are located a number of the largest and most famous of the Adirondack hotels, prominent among them being the Algonquin.

No illustration can convey to the reader the beauty of the location of this hotel, situated as it is on the lower Saranac Lake, one of the most beautiful of the Adirondack gems. There are few, if any, locations in the North Woods where one may find amid such delightful natural surroundings such a comfortable and luxurious hotel. Nothing is lacking that will increase the comfort of its guests.

There is most excellent sport to be had in the neighborhood of the Algonquin, and the fishing in the Saranac is too famous to need particular mention here.

Further information regarding this region may be had of Mr. John Harding, Algonquin P. O., Franklin Co., N. Y.

Some man with a keen sense of humor has said that the Chateaugay Railroad, which, having its beginning at Plattsburg, penetrates the most delightful portion of the Adirondacks, should be called the "Bee Line," because its course is so like that of the busy bee, flitting from flower to flower. There is a wonderful degree of freshness and variety in the scenery along this picturesque line: towering mountains hem in the horizon on each side, while here and there the valleys

hundreds from gratifying their desire to visit them, but most of the choicer places are now easily reached by the Chateaugay Railroad via Plattsburg. The lakes along this line include such gems as Upper and Lower Chateaugay, Chazy, Loon, Rainbow and the Upper and Lower Saranac. On the two latter the finest trip by water of any in the whole North Woods is to be enjoyed. Comfortably seated in one of the light Adirondack boats with a strong-armed guide at the oars, one may start at the Algonquin and skirt the lily-padded and wooded shore of the entire Lower Saranac, and by making a short "carry," he may launch his craft in the Upper Saranac. From here he may by turns cross the placid bosom of

open out, disclosing vistas of lovely lakes, skirted to the very edges with dense forests of pine tree and balsam. There is not

It is a paradise for the lover of the rod and gun.

a mile of the Chateaugay Railroad which is not full of interest to even the casual tourist, and it reaches hotels of all grades, from elegant, thoroughly equipped houses where the wealthy and fashionable may enjoy every luxury, to the more modest but comfortable resort where people of the most moderate means find delightful summer homes. In the earlier days of the Adirondack mountains as a summer resort the long, tedious stage road necessary to reach distant points prevented

Fish Creek, Big Square, Floodwood, Rollins and Whey ponds, all lovely bodies of water edged with forest-covered mountains. It is one of the most beautiful trips imaginable, and to the lover of nature an ideal way to spend a half week. In fact no one can fully appreciate the most fascinating phases and hidden beauties of Adirondack life until he has taken this most romantic of trips by boat, for Nature hides her choicest gems in the deepest recesses of the mountains, apart from the beaten paths of man.

to the railroad that the New York markets are drawn upon very liberally for the table supplies, and the surrounding country furnishes an abundance of fresh vegetables, fruit and milk. There are in the Wawbeck all the conveniences which the most exacting guests may require, and it is in the very centre of the best fishing and shooting districts of the North

There are many spots on the route where the forests descend to the water's edge and the eye cannot penetrate the tangled growth. Their mysterious perfume embodies the deepest, sweetest, most delightful secrets of nature; the odor is subtle, fragrant beyond description, and heavy with aromatic airs.

The Adirondack "guides," in the Saranac, and other sections of the woods, are as fine a set of men as can be found the world over. As a rule they are thoroughly sober, trustworthy, willing and companionable, and can shoot, cook, and tell yarns with a skill truly remarkable. They know the great trackless wilderness thoroughly, and the writer has never in his experience seen, and then but for a moment, one puzzled over his location but once, and that was when making a "carry" from one pond to an-

"An Incident of the chase."

Woods. The largest trout catch of the past season was made in this lake a short distance from the Hotel Wawbeck shore. A post-office and telegraph-office are in the house, and various delightful trips may be made from this point, by either land or water. Send to the manager. Wawbeck N. Y., for pamphlet regarding the attractions of this ideal region.

"The carry between the Saranac Lakes is a short one."

other on a dark night through an almost impenetrable forest.

On the shores of the upper Saranac Lake stands the Hotel Wawbeck with its cottages. The Wawbeck is not a sanitarium, but is intended to be, and is, a delightfully situated, beautifully run and thoroughly ideal summer home. Mr. Harlow H. Chandler has been its manager for three seasons, and has impressed not only his popularity, but that of the house, effectually upon all his guests. The Wawbeck is so conveniently located

"Few return empty-handed."

Chateaugay Lake has for many years been the favorite rendezvous of those who wish to combine fishing and hunting with the many other attractive features of the North Woods. Nowhere are there greater or better opportunities for sport. The entire region about Chateaugay and Chazy

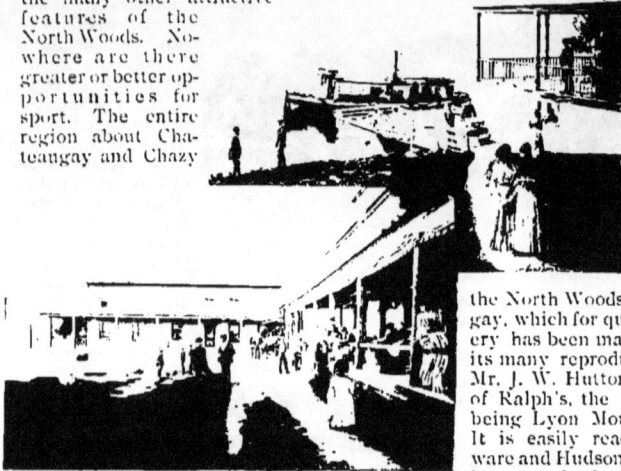

"Good health and wholesome pleasure go hand in hand at Ralph's."

Lakes, and in fact along the line of the Chateaugay railroad, is a natural game and fish preserve where excellent sport is sure to be had.

One of the famous resorts whose name is almost indissolubly associated with the Adirondacks is Ralph's, on the eastern shore of the Chateaugay Lake, about three and one-half miles over a good road from the railroad station at Lyon Mountain on the Chateaugay Railroad. It is in the heart of the delightfully wild region, where the throbbings of the great wilderness are most distinct. Ralph's is one of those fascinating, home-like spots,

"The Chateaugay Hotel stands on the north shore of the Lake."

where, if one goes for a week, he is tempted to linger for a month. Good health and wholesome pleasure here go hand in hand, and each season finds at Ralph's many old and familiar faces who have found in Chateaugay Lake and at this famous hotel the ideal of contentment and comfort. There will be found at Ralph's all of the accompanying conveniences and excellent fishing, with game in abundance. As for boating, there is no more inviting lake in the North Woods than the Chateaugay, which for quiet beauty of scenery has been made famous through its many reproductions on canvas. Mr. J. W. Hutton is the proprietor of Ralph's, the post-office address being Lyon Mountain, New York. It is easily reached by the Delaware and Hudson Railroad to Plattsburg, and the Chateaugay Railroad from there to Lyon Mountain.

The Chateaugay Hotel, which stands on the north shore of the beautiful lake from which it takes its name, commands a most attractive view, east, south, and west. Mr. Charles W. Backus, the proprietor, purchased it in 1893, and has spared neither money, pains, nor labor, to make it as attractive and comfortable a hostelry as can be found in the Adirondacks.

On the eastern side of Lake Champlain is the pretty city of Burlington, with its 20,000 inhabitants, its college, its scores of magnificent residences, its extensive manufactories, and its many historical associations. Here the lake is at its widest, and one may look westward across its lovely surface and see the Adirondack Mountains, a sea of stern and rugged peaks, silhouetted against the sky, while to the east rise the rounded slopes of the Green Mountains. Burlington has been aptly called "the Naples of the midland sea" by one of the many poets who have sung its charms, while another writer has said that it has the mountain scenery of Scotland, the sky and sunsets of Italy, the valleys and verdure of France, the lake views of Switzerland, with the park-like surroundings of an English landscape.

At Port Kent, 54 miles from Ticonderoga, connection may be made by tourists with the new railroad to the famous Ausable Chasm, three miles beyond.

This masterpiece of nature, which Baedecker pronounced the greatest natural wonder in America, after Niagara Falls, is impressive beyond description, and the pictures which are presented tell of its grandeur and beauty more graphically than would be possible in words.

From far up in the mountain fastnesses the two forks of the Ausable River have come by tortuous and uncertain courses through inviting valleys until they meet just below the picturesque Memington Pass. Then uniting they join in a mad rush for Lake Champlain, making almost at the very start a magnificent plunge over Alice Falls, the most beautiful in the Adirondacks.

This splendid cataract falls about forty feet, much of it being an almost sheer fall over ledges of rock with magnificent foaming watery stairways bordering it with their delicate lace work on either hand. The water, of which there is a large volume, tumbles down into an immense amphitheatre, which has been rounded by the torrent out of the adjacent enclosing rocks during past ages, and emerging flows sharply to the right, over some rapids, and then over a prosaic mill-dam, which is built across just above the chasm. Suddenly, as if to try its powers, the river leaps over a short fall,

and then with a force and majesty which is overpowering plunges seventy feet into the deep abyss below. Clouds of spray float upward to be tinted with all the colors of the rainbow by the summer's sun.

The trip through the chasm is one of constant surprises. Nature has disported herself here in her wildest mood. Sheer precipices, nearly 150 feet high, terminate in deep, dark pools where the water rests after its tumultous passage through the more narrow gorges. There are many interesting and wonderful spots to be passed as the visitor follows the narrow pathway cleft in the sides of the dripping walls. They bear all kinds of fantastic names as best befit their own local surroundings. The most impressive sensation of the trip is reserved for the end. The visitor, seated in a long boat and guided by a boatman who handles the paddle, shoots the rapids at the foot of the cliffs 200 feet high. passing through one point where the river is but 13 feet wide. Looking back one seems to be plunging downhill. The boat darts through a flume about a quarter of a mile long and emerges into a broad placid basin which marks the exit from the chasm, from which the widened river flows through a flat open country until it empties into Lake Champlain.

The Lake View House at the Chasm and the Chasm itself are under the management of Mr. W. H. Tracy.

"Baedecker pronounces this chasm to be the greatest natural wonder in America next to the Niagara Falls."

"In the Ausable Chasm Nature has disported herself in her wildest moods."

From Port Kent the stately steamer *Vermont* follows on its trip the western shore of the lake, passing the picturesque Ausable Point, and between Valcour Island and the bluffs, touches at Bluff Point, the landing-place of the great Hotel Champlain, which fittingly crowns a noble promontory overlooking the lake and the mountains far beyond. This house is typical in the highest sense of the perfection to which American architects and capitalists have brought the summer hotel. It is surrounded

ful, it being simply a choice as between lake and mountain. The purest of mountain spring water is brought from the far-away reservoirs of nature, and the winds which are wafted from the recesses of the mountains are laden with the very purity of heaven.

Immediately below the hotel is an abrupt, wooded declivity, a bit of the clean sandy beach, showing at the foot of an open swath cut through the firs. To the northward is Cumberland Bay, and across Cumberland Head the further waters of the lake near its foot. A mile away, intermediate, is Crab Island and to the right Valcour Island, checkered with farms and belted with forest area.

by a beautiful natural park of 450 acres of woodland and meadow, and more than $50,000 has been spent in constructing

"The great Hotel Champlain fittingly crowns a noble promontory overlooking the lake."

under a well-devised plan perfect roadways, lawns, and walks along the lake shore, cliffs, and forests, the house itself being built upon a foundation of solid rock. Each one of its nearly half-thousand rooms commands a view of surpassing loveliness. There are no back rooms in this house, because there is a frontage to each point of the compass, and the outlooks afforded are all beauti-

Five miles across is Grand Isle, and beyond to the eastward and southeast the shore of Vermont, purple in the evening shadows long before the sun fades from the flanks of the Green Mountains. To the right the view of the lake is clear for twenty miles; away down below Burlington to the narrow reach of the southern extreme there are scores of distant islands, which now and then gloom in passing cloud-shadows and again are lost in the dim shore line behind.

White smoke-plumes sway and rise and fade along the western shore, where express trains, themselves unseen and unheard, speed along the rocky reaches around the headlands miles away upon the "D. & H." Swift steamboats break the still surface, and loitering sail-craft wait for the evening breeze. Over the lake the eye continuously travels upward to the base of the rugged steeps of Mt. Mansfield and all of its group of lesser peaks. To sit here in this broad proscenium watching a sunrise is a poem; to look at it in eventide is an epic.

The interior finishing and furnishing of the house are luxurious and bear out the fair promise of the tasteful white and gray exterior so set off by the long spacious porches overlooking the lake. Mr. O. D. Seavey, whose name is so very long associated with the Ponce de Leon at Saint Augustine, is, and has been since its opening, the manager of this hotel. This in itself is an assurance that nothing which can tend to increase the pleasure or comfort of the guests will be overlooked.

Life at the Hotel Champlain involves a most extraordinary variety of diversions. Equestrian expeditions are possible in various directions, and pedestrian wanderings are exceedingly popular. Frequent steamboats upon the lake and local trains upon the railroad offer a long list of single-day excursions, each enjoyable in its turn. Much of the best fishing

"White smoke-plumes rise and fade along the western shore, where express trains speed along the rocky reaches."

and hunting territory of the Adirondack region may be reached in time to enjoy a good day's sport and return at nightfall. Lake Placid, the most widely known resort in the Adirondack Mountains, is easily accessible from Bluff Point. The abundant provision for thoroughly heating the house in the late season makes the Hotel Champlain a most desirable point for gentlemen sportsmen to locate their families during the autumn gunning period. Billiard tables and a series of bowling alleys (in a separate structure) offer a remedy for ennui in inclement weather.

The largest military post in the East is close by, and adds greatly to the social attractions of the place, with its drills, guard mounts, and dress parades. The music is furnished by Brooks' Band and Orchestra, and the ballroom is nightly a scene of gayety and pleasure. Fort Montgomery, Fort Ethan Allen, and the historical ruins of the forts at Crown Point and Ticonderoga are near by. All the steamers and the Champlain Transportation Company and all the trains of the D. & H. stop at the Hotel Champlain, the pier being at the foot of the bluff and the station in the park just west of the hotel. The Hotel Champlain is thus easy of access, in either drawing-room or sleeping-car from New York, Albany, or Saratoga. It is a natural and convenient stopping-point for tourists making the trip to or from Montreal, the Adirondacks, the White Mountains, or Lake Champlain points.

Bluff Point is also the station for the Catholic Summer School of America, an institution whose usefulness is conceded and whose success is assured. The press, Catholic and non-Catholic, has been lavish in its praise. It has been duly incorporated by a charter from the Regents of the University of New York,

pany, whose officers are such well-known financiers as John Byrne, John D. Crimmins, Daniel O'Day, Thomas F. Ryan, Adrian Iselin, Jr., of New York, and Martin Maloney, of Philadelphia, is engaged in developing this property. A comprehensive topographical survey and complete plan have been made by the eminent engineer and sanitary expert, Col. George E. Waring, Jr. It is in contemplation to provide for about one thousand summer cottages.

A perfect system of sewage, water supply, and lighting has been planned. The grounds have been systematically laid out in the most attractive

" A casino, or administration building, immediately adjoins the delightful park."

and is regularly and officially classified within the system of public instruction devoted to university extension.

The Catholic Summer School aims to increase the facilities for busy people as well as for those of leisure to pursue lines of study in various departments of knowledge by providing opportunities of getting instruction from eminent specialists. It is not intended to have the scope of the work limited to any class, but rather to establish an intellectual centre where any one with serious purpose, in the leisure of a summer vacation, without great expense, may come and find new incentives to efforts for self-improvement. All branches of human learning, history, literature, natural and theological science, are to be considered in the light of Christian truth, according to Cardinal Newman's declaration: " Truth is the object of knowledge of whatever kind; and truth means facts and their relations. Religious truth is not only a portion, but a condition of knowledge. To blot it out is nothing short of unravelling the web of university teaching."

Through the liberality of the Delaware and Hudson Railroad corporation, the Catholic Summer School owns a magnificent estate of four hundred and fifty acres, situated on the west shore of Lake Champlain. The Catholic Summer School Building and Improvement Com-

manner by means of winding roads, and the preservation of the stately forest groves, natural elevations, and particularly pleasing trees. A deep and picturesque ravine, traversing about one-third of the property, running almost west and east, and carrying a crystal brook in its bed, affords a delightful landscape effect; while the thickly wooded bluff, with its delightful glades and sheltered nooks, overlooking the waters of the majestic Champlain, and the tree-covered border of the lake itself, with meandering syl-

" Commanding views of the most magnificent expanse of the lake with its beautiful islands."

van paths, affording charming surprises and many varying views of the shimmering water and distant mountains, form two natural rambles over half a mile in length, calculated to delight the tourist's eye and lure him into their leafy shades. Rustic chairs and tables, and pretty summer houses perched on rugged bluff or on grassy knoll, increase the comfort of visitors.

There has been erected a handsome Assembly and Administration Building, which serves as a club house for the Board of Trustees and the honorary members of the Association, and will give luncheon accommodations to cottagers and visitors.

John Lafarge, LL.D., Rev. J. A. Zahm, Ph.D., C. S. C., Notre Dame University, Henry Austin Adams, A. M., Rev. Hermann Heuser, St. Charles' Seminary, Rev. W. H. O'Connell, Brother Baldwin, Rev. J. A. Doonan, S. J., Rev. Henry G. Ganss, Lawrence D. Flick, M.D., Rev. D. J. O'Sullivan.

"Where the scenery is rugged and the cliffs severe."

The Summer School affords an ideal place for a summer vacation. Its location is superb. It is easily accessible from New York and from the principal large cities. It affords every opportunity for rest and healthful recreation of all kinds—boating, fishing, bathing, walking, riding, driving, mountain climbing. Besides thus enabling one to pass a vacation in *otio cum dig.*, it will keep his imagination and mind pleasantly occupied. The Rev. Thos. J. Conaty, D.D., of Worcester, Mass., is President, the Rev. F. P. Siegfried, of Philadelphia, Chairman of the Board of Studies, and the Chairman of the Executive Committee is the Hon. John B. Riley, Plattsburg, N. Y.

The session of 1895 will open with Pontifical Mass, on July 7, Archbishop Satolli celebrant, and the sermon delivered by Archbishop Corrigan. The courses will include ecclesiastical history, literature, science and art. The lecturers are Very Rev. John B. Hogan, S.S., D.D., Rev. J. F. Loughlin, D.D., George Parsons Lathrop, LL.D., Rev. T. J. A. Freeman, S. J., Condé B. Pallen, Ph.D., Richard Malcolm Johnston, LL.D.,

Besides Archbishop Corrigan the other preachers of the session will be Most Rev. P. J. Ryan, D.D., Archbishop of Philadelphia, Rt. Rev. Thomas D. Beaven, D.D., Bishop of Springfield, Mass., Rt. Rev. T. S. Byrne, D.D., Bishop of Nashville, Tenn., Rev. P. J. Garrigan, D.D., Vice-Rector Catholic University of America, Rev. Thomas J. Conaty, D.D., Rev. Clarence E. Woodman, Ph.D., C.S.P., Rev. J. Coyle, Rev. J. M. Whelan, Very Rev. J. F. Mooney, D.D., V.G., New York, Rev. J. L. Belford. More detailed information may be obtained by addressing WARREN E. MOSHER, Secretary, 123 E. 50th St., New York City.

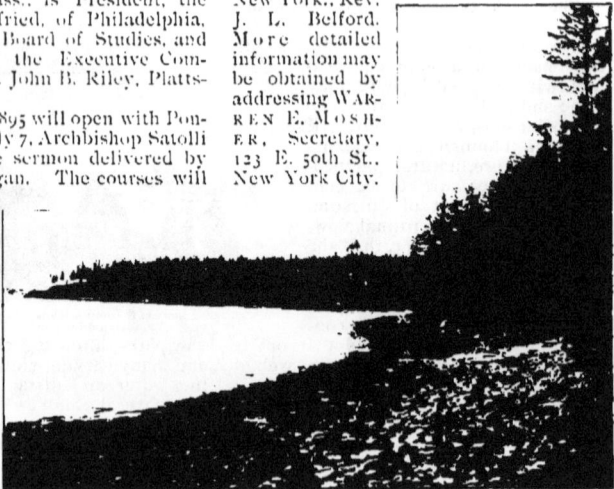

"Wide stretches of pebbly beach, where the waves lap caressingly."

Plattsburg, three miles beyond Bluff Point, is the terminal point of the steamers which run from Fort Ticonderoga. It is a beautiful little city of eight or ten thousand inhabitants, a county-seat, and is attractively located on the shore of Lake Champlain just where the Saranac River empties into it. The views which are given convey some impression of the attractive features of Plattsburg. Among its fine buildings are the United States Custom House and Post Office, St. Peter's Church, and a quaint old French nunnery. South of the town a mile is the United States Barracks.

Plattsburg is connected with the early history of the country as being the place where Macdonough and Macomb defeated the British naval and land

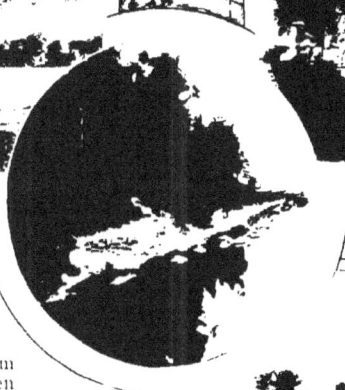

" Every mile of Champlain's shores is picturesque."

forces under Commodore Downie and Sir George Provost. The American navy on Lake Champlain consisted at that time of the men-of-war *Saratoga, Eagle, Ticonderoga,* and *Preble,* carrying from 7 to 26 guns, and a dozen smaller gunboats. The British fleet consisted of the *Confiance,* carrying 38 guns, the *Linnet, Chub,* and *Finch,* and 12 smaller gunboats. As the first gun was fired from the British fleet, Gen. Provost with 14,000 troops assaulted the town of Plattsburg, which was garrisoned by 3,000 men under Gen. Macomb. The fight was a stubborn one on land and lake, and the British were finally repulsed with a loss of about

2,500 men and an immense amount of baggage and ammunition, while the American force lost less than 150. The British Commodore Downie was killed early in the fight, and the American Commodore Macdonough was crushed to the deck of his vessel by a falling boom which had been cut off by a cannon-ball. A number of the infantry killed in this battle are buried in the Plattsburg Cemetery, while the men of the fleets who were killed are buried on Crab Island.

"The Witherill House is delightfully embowered in trees."

The tourist stopping at Plattsburg will find in the Witherill Hotel an exceptionally comfortable and well-appointed house, excellently kept and attractively furnished. It is centrally located in the most delightful part of Plattsburg, and is a popular rendezvous for tourists going in or out of the Adirondacks.

Rouse's Point, the next important place on the lake above Plattsburg, marks the Canadian territory. It is a brisk little village of 1,500 inhabitants at the mouth of the Richelieu River—through which the explorer, Champlain, came in his canoe when he first gazed upon the lake which has ever since borne his name and which to-day alone perpetuates it. Fort Montgomery, one mile north of the place, commands the Richelieu River with 164 guns.

An unfortunate mistake was made in the location of this fort, and after a large amount of money was spent it was found to be built on British territory and was abandoned; it was given the ironical name of Fort Blunder. Subsequently, however, a change in the boundary line gave the land to the United States, and the fort was completed at the expense of over half a million of dollars.

If the tourist seeks the best grounds for fishing he will find them among the islands in the northern end of the lake. Here bass and pickerel abound, and here are the sites of many camping parties. From these islands delightful views are obtained of the Green Mountains, from Jay Peak at the north to the dim outlines of Mount Mansfield on the south. St. Albans appears on the distant hillside. All about are islands too rocky for camping purposes—having such titles as Diadama, Hen, Old Woman, and Pop Squash—while a little farther up the shore we are soothed with Balm of Gilead Point. Close by, and strung along the shore, is "the city"—the only cluster of buildings on all of the fifty or more islands in the lake—and looking very like "the Huddle" at Lake George.

The passage through the Gut is only a mile or so in length, but every rod of it shows new phases of island beauty. Bow-Arrow Point, at the southern end of North Hero, well bears out its title. Outside the passage, and between The Sisters and South Hero, a glorious view of the Adirondacks bursts upon one in all the majesty of its unequalled grandeur.

The Champlain Transportation Company, which operates the beautiful steamers on Lake Champlain, is one of the best-equipped steamship companies in America. The *Vermont* and the *Chateaugay* make daily round trips in connection with the trains of the Delaware and Hudson Railroad. These steamers are large, modern, and of sufficiently heavy burden to accommodate one thousand people. It is beyond question that upon no inland lake in the world

"Here bass and pickerel abound and afford rare sport."

is the passenger service more promptly attended to or the tourists more satisfactorily cared for than upon the steamers of this line.

"The Rhine, the St. Lawrence, and the Hudson," said Bayard Taylor, "are the three most beautiful rivers of the

" In olden days the rapids were shot in boats, now in stately steamers "

world," and while each has its individual charms, the St. Lawrence in many ways is entitled to the place of honor. The Richelieu and Ontario Navigation Company has made it possible, by placing in service a fleet of palatial steamboats, for the tourist to enjoy every portion of it, and in addition he may go far up its chief tributary, the world-renowned Saguenay, the natural grandeur of whose scenery no pen has yet adequately portrayed. The route of the steamers from their western terminus takes one through the Thousand Islands, affording panoramic views of this natural paradise of water and verdure, as the steamer threads its way amid the labyrinth of islands, more than 1,700 in number. After the noble river has extricated itself from the islands, it begins to increase its current, and finally with turbulent

lashing plunges down the famous Lachine rapids. The trip through these rapids is an exhilarating experience never to be forgotten. While there is the maximum of excitement, there is the minimum of danger, though the experience is often trying to the nerves, especially when the steamboat makes a lurch in the chaotic waters and a volume of spray is dashed in the faces of the thrilled voyagers.

To the eastward of Montreal and Quebec, both of which cities are reached by the boats of the Richelieu and Ontario, the journey by river is none the less interesting. The steamers touch at Rivière du Loup, near the famous watering-place Cacouna, and then crossing the river, which is here about twenty miles wide, stop at Tadousac before beginning the ascent of the Saguenay.

" The Grand Discharge on Lake St. John is fascinating to all who see it."

The commercial metropolis of Canada, Montreal, occupies a magnificent position, facing the broad St. Lawrence on the one side and receding toward the beautiful Mt. Royal on the other, upon the summit and sides of which is the lovely Mountain Park, which has added much to Montreal's fair fame. The view from the summit of this mountain, which is reached by broad

"Montreal with its tree-embowered squares and evidences of prosperity."

roads over easy grades, is one of the most sublime of any of this continent.

Far below and spreading out upon all sides, in grand and solid proportions, with broad-paved avenues, maple-adorned streets, brilliant squares, open parks, hundreds of spires, cupolas, and domes, and high above all, rising conspicuously, the huge towers of Notre Dame and the colossal form of St. Peter's, one may behold the Montreal of to-day. Montreal with its wealth and its poverty, its grandeur and its beauty, its wonderful paintings, its museums, galleries, and libraries; its vast warehouses, its rush and noise; yet not a sound ascending from its life-filled streets. Away to the right is to be seen the famed canal and the world-renowned rapids. Lower down, stretched across the broad St. Lawrence, the Victoria Bridge flings its huge proportions, its diminishing tail touching the shore at St. Lambert and its monster head swallowing up a train that rushes from St. Cunégonde into its iron jaws.

The city of Montreal has a full complement of hotels; but the Balmoral on Notre Dame Street, one block from Victoria Square and five minutes' walk from the steamboat and railway stations, will be found a thoroughly enjoyable hotel home. Messrs. E. H. Dunham & Company, the proprietors, are well known as thoroughly alert and alive to the requirements of the better class of the travelling public. $75,000 has recently been spent on the Balmoral, and it is now as complete, well-furnished and cheerful a house as there is in Canada. The extensive corridors and drawing-rooms of the Balmoral make the house especially desirable for ladies and children, and its location makes it peculiarly well adapted for visitors who desire to view the many and delightful points of interest in Montreal. Electric cars of every line in Montreal pass the hotel door, and for this very reason it is a convenient house at which to make headquarters. Tourist parties may secure accommodations in

The Balmoral Hotel at Montreal makes a specialty of pleasing tourists."

advance by telegraph, and will receive every consideration. The Balmoral is conducted on the American plan.

In quaint, delightful, and moss-covered old Quebec, so rich in historical associations and fascinating traditions of dead and gone heroes, English, French, and aboriginal, there is so much of interest to see and hear that if the tourist's sojourn within its gates—in this case the gates are actual—is to be of short duration, he must be up and doing, or going, early and late, for there is a wealth of historical and legendary facts and fancies from which to glean. Quebec is unique, first, in that it has been the scene of more war and strife than any other city on the western continent, and again because of its impressive location. Here have transpired a long succession of events in which the vital interests of great nations were involved, supremacy being attained only by fierce and terrible battle. The natural splendor of the city's surroundings could scarcely be excelled. It is truly a "city set upon a hill," standing guard over the entrance to the great inland waters of the continent; the fortress-crowned rock with its grim armament which overlooks the river and the Lower

"In quaint, delightful, and moss-covered Quebec there is much to see."

Town has earned for it the title of the American Gibraltar.

On the banks of the St. Lawrence,

"Its fortifications overlooking the old town below."

where Quebec now sits in her beauty and majesty, there stood three hundred and fifty-nine years ago a small Indian village. Here it was that Cartier anchored his fleet about 1536, and claimed it, and whatever else there may have been thereabouts, as the possession of the King of France. He did nothing, however, toward building up a settlement, and it was not until 1608, when Champlain arrived and established French ownership, that it began to grow to make history. For some time thereafter Champlain practically reigned as King of the St. Lawrence and exercised an absolute sovereignty over the territory from the Gulf of Mexico to Canada.

The Plains of Abraham, a table-land on the summit of the heights on the north bank of the St. Lawrence, were thought to have been too precipitous to be reached by an enemy. But history tells us how

"The city gates of Quebec are not fanciful but real."

the plain was reached and was the scene of the desperate and terrific battle which decided the possession of Canada. It was on that fateful day that Wolfe died at the very moment of his victory, and Montcalm received mortal wounds. A monument to Wolfe's valiant leadership has been erected here, and in the Governor's Garden is a dual-faced monument, raised in 1827 to the joint honor of these two heroes, and bearing the inscription "Valor gave a common death, history a common fame, and posterity a common monument." On the plains, reached by a picturesque old stairway from the Lower Town, are three towers, erected in 1812 for the city's defence.

The Citadel has the most commanding position in the city, being

"The Montmorency plunges 250 feet into the chasm below."

303 feet above the water, and is said to contain arms sufficient to equip 20,000 men.

The gates of the city are three in number and stand at its western approach. St. John's gate is, however, the only one of the three that is at all ancient. The foundation-stone of the Kent gate was laid by the Princess Louise while residing in Canada when her husband, the Marquis of Lorne, was Governor-General. The gate is named in honor of the father of Queen Victoria, who at one time was in command of the British forces in Canada. The third gate, the St. Louis, is near the Government buildings.

One of the most delightful places at Quebec for the tourist to make his

"One of the delightful places for the tourist to stop at is the Florence."

home for a longer or shorter period is the Hotel Florence, a picture of which is presented on this page. The location of the Florence is one of the most attractive, from a natural standpoint, in the quaint old city in which it is so prominent and popular. There is to be had from its balcony a wide-stretching and beautiful panoramic view of the St. Lawrence River and the city. This view, which includes not only the beautiful Falls of Montmorency, the Laurentian Range of mountains, and the lovely valley of the St. Charles, is not surpassed even from the renowned Dufferin Terrace. The location of the Florence is very convenient to all the prominent places of interest, and street-cars reaching every portion of the city pass the door every five minutes. The interior finishings and furnishings of the Florence are new and elegant, and thoroughly in keeping with the general excellence and reputation of the house. The markets of Quebec are famous for the great variety of sea-foods and vegetables, and the table of the

Florence offers a most excellent opportunity to test the high reputation of these delicacies, as the *cuisine* is up to the highest standard. The house is lighted with electricity, every room being supplied, and there are on each floor iron balconies and iron doors, thus insuring perfect safety. Mr. Benjamin Trudel presides over the Florence as both proprietor and manager, and also over the new and modern Victoria, one of the finest hotels in Canada. The tourist stopping at either of these delightful houses will be well pleased.

The tourist from the United States

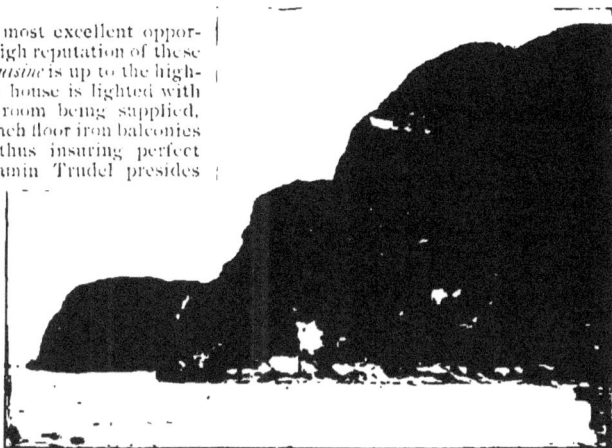

"What pen has ever conveyed the faintest impression of the awful majesty of Capes Trinity and Eternity on the Saguenay River?"

who visits Quebec without taking the trip up the wonderful Saguenay River is turning away from, at its very threshold, the most magnificent scenery—the Yellowstone and Yosemite of Canada combined. Who can paint in words or on canvass the glories of the Saguenay! What pen has ever conveyed anything but faintest impression of the yawning and awful majesty of Cape Eternity, that tremendous cliff 1,500 feet in height, or its neighbor, Cape Trinity, showing its three distinct heads both vertical and lateral! The entire trip of the Saguenay River, from Tadousac, where it joins the St. Lawrence, to Chicoutimi, fascinates and overawes one. Mr. W. H. H. Murray, in describing it, says: "It is a monstrous cleft opened by earthquake violence for sixty miles through a landscape of mountains formed of primeval rocks. In old time a shock which shook the world burst the Laurentian range asunder at its St. Lawrence line, where Tadousac now is, and opened up a chasm, two

miles across, two thousand feet in depth, and sixty miles in length, straight northward. Thus was the Saguenay born." The beautiful steamers of the Richelieu and Ontario Navigation Company are modern and commodious, and the comforts and luxuries of travel are provided upon them. There are along the route several interesting little towns, and every portion of the distance has its peculiar charms. At Chicoutimi connection is made with the Quebec and Lake St. John Railroad for Roberval on Lake St. John, which is the source of the Saguenay, and one of the most delightful lakes to visit on the American Continent. It has become in recent years the Mecca of the tourist, sportsman, and woodsman. The main line of the Quebec and Lake St. John Railroad is between Quebec and Lake St. John and the distance is but one hundred and ninety miles, and through an interesting region of mountain fastnesses, yawning chasms, and natural parks.

Some appreciation of the great beauty and magnitude of this region may be shown in the statement that there are within the confines of the Triton Fishing and Gun Club reservation more than 200 lakes of a mile, or over, long, with a myriad connecting streams, all abounding in trout, salmon, and ouananiche, the great fighter of the north. Tourists are enabled to make the round trip from Quebec, going to Lake St. John by water, over the St. Lawrence and Saguenay rivers, and returning by rail, or vice versa.

At Lake St. John, one is sur-

"One finds at Roberval on Lake St. John a handsome hotel."

prised to find, in the Roberval, situated on the western shore of the lake, a splendid modern hotel large enough to accommodate three hundred guests, equipped with everything that the most fastidious could desire for physical comfort and well-being. The interior furnishings are new, and very great taste has been exercised in their selection. The house has all such modernisms as electric lights and bells, and is supplied with every facility for indoor amusement, such as billiards, bowling, dancing, etc. The grounds surrounding it are brilliantly lighted by electricity at night, and, in addition to the splendid boating, fishing and driving, there are beautiful tennis courts. The views afforded of Lake St. John from the windows of this house are exceedingly beautiful. The earliest ouananiche fishing is to be had immediately in front of the Roberval, usually about the first week in June, while the most exciting sport with this gamiest of fresh-water fish is to be had between the first week in July and the middle of September. The Island House, under the same management, situated on an island of the Grand Discharge, and reached in about two hours by steamer from the Roberval, is a most comfortable hotel and much sought by those who wish to fish from canoes. Here the ouananiche is to be found in shoals, waiting to spring on his favorite fly as soon as it is afloat, and the Canadian *voyageurs* will paddle one about very skilfully amid the dangerous rocks and whirling eddies.

The proprietors of the Roberval and Island House have the exclusive fishing rights of Lake St. John and its tributaries. These waters, however, are free to the guests at these hotels.

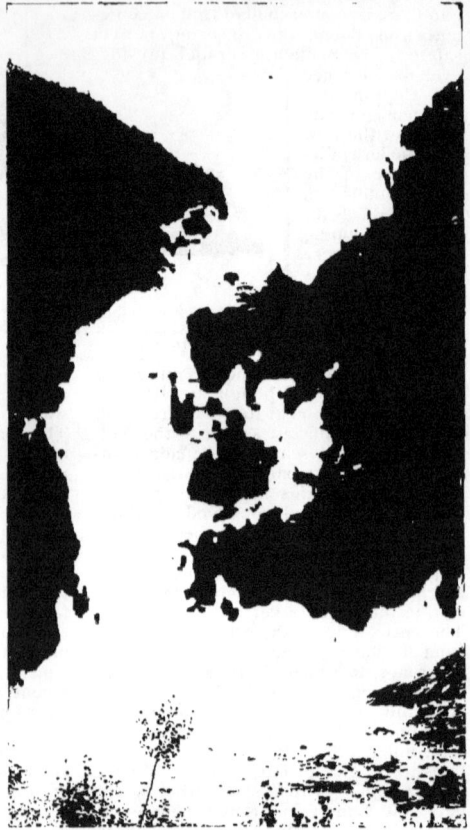

"The magnificent spectacle of Ouatchouan Falls, higher by a hundred feet than Niagara."

The pleasures of camping in this region need no recommendation to those who have once tried them. There are from fifteen to twenty routes mapped out, which were unknown to white men up to three or four years ago. The inland streams and lakes northward that form such enjoyable links in the chain of these tours abound with trout, their waters having scarcely ever been invaded by civilized fishermen. Large game of all kinds is plentiful.

This territory forms the northernmost limits of "A Summer Paradise."

"The hurrying waters of the Lightning River."